Companality®

Developing Intentional Organizational Culture

Tom –
Congrats on running
a great company!

– Steve Fales

9/4/19

Companality®

Developing Intentional Organizational Culture

A brief how-to manual for creating the
unique intangible characteristics that leaders
desire in the organizations they serve.

Steve Fales

Published by Praeter Advisory 🄿

Companality: Developing Intentional Organizational Culture

© 2019 by Steven H. Fales

Published by Praeter Advisory, Florida.

Edited by Alan Williamson

Cover Design by Charlie Masella

Interior Layout by Charlie Masella

Printed in the United States of America

ISBN 978-1-7331446-0-5

To JR StJohn.

Contents

Acknowledgments

This book is all about the workplace environment. I owe a debt of gratitude to many who have made my own corporate experience reflect the proper culture.

- Tonya and Gregg, true Companality champions.
- Stephanie and Tonya, who took care of all the details.
- Alan, talented contributor and editor.
- Charlie, for bearing with multiple rounds of revisions.
- And all the people of AdServices Inc., present and past, who have agreed to buy in to the Companality.

With sincere appreciation,

Steve Fales

Introduction

A business consists of both tangible and intangible elements. The tangibles are easy to comprehend. Office space, desks, computers, phones, marketing materials, and the like. The intangibles, however, are a bit more obscure by their very definition.

Invisible as they might be, every time we interact with an organization, we know those factors are at work. The broad term for what's going on beneath the surface has been called "culture." I invented a more descriptive word: Companality.

Just as a person has a personality, a company has a Companality. And my claim is that this goes for any type of organization – small, large, commercial, non-profit – you name it. Every organization, I believe, has a Companality.

It's my further opinion that Companality has a great many effects on the entity that it embodies. The type of customer and employee the firm attracts, and its reputation are all downstream of culture.

Sadly, most organizations' cultures come about in ways that the leadership never endorsed, resulting in a Companality they may not find desirable. The good news is that a Companality CAN be developed intentionally, aiming toward and achieving a pre-defined purpose, with individual components positively aligned.

Once the vision is clear, there's a specific process for making it reality, and for getting it to permeate the organization from the C-suite to the front lines. The process requires commitment, but it works no matter the size or scope of the organization involved.

And there you have an overview of the Companality story. Now it's time to dig deeper into the why and how; and the nuts and bolts of execution that make this all happen.

Here's to intentionally-developed organizational cultures wherever this book is read.

Steve Fales

1

Encounters
With
Companality

You're about to read a few sets of words that will invite you to share a hypothetical experience. As you see each statement, pause to note your reaction and any feelings that surface. Let's start.

We're going on a little adventure.

> (Are you intrigued? Excited? Curious?)

But we'll have to stand in line.

> (Any reaction?)

To get into Disney World.

> (What are you feeling?)

Sorry, change of plans ... It's to get your driver's license renewed.

> (How about now?)

Think about your response to each statement? Most likely, your thoughts about going to Disney World were much different than those about getting your driver's license renewed. Why is that?

No doubt visiting a major theme park holds a greater promise of fun than a trip to the local government office, but the reasons for the disparity in your emotions run deeper than that. Experience and observation have conditioned us to have certain expectations about these places. We see one as inviting, exciting, and full of joy. We see the other as drab, painfully slow, and totally apathetic to us as humans. These experiences are uncannily consistent.

The reason for this is simple. It's because every business, government office, non-profit, institution, or enterprise of any kind has its own unique organizational culture.

Think of it like this. People all have their own individual characteristics. We refer to this as personality. Likewise, companies and organizations have distinct characteristics. This we call Companality.

A person has a personality. A company has a Companality.

2

Companality
And
Organizational Culture

Companality is the culture of an organization, and it applies to any kind of entity.

What is organizational culture? Let's start with an academic definition, then break it down.

Organizational culture is
a combination of characteristics shared across an organization that dictate the experience of both customers and team members as they interact with that organization.

Now let's look at each piece of the definition individually, starting with the first phrase:

... a combination of characteristics ...

There are many characteristics that contribute to an organization's culture. The ones we'll consider are:

Attitudes
Values
Morals
Work/Life Ethic

Attitudes

An attitude is an outlook, a way of viewing people, ideas, environments and situations. Attitudes are generally thought to be either positive or negative, and often nothing more. While that is a good start, there are bigger truths to be considered, as attitudes can be revealed via many nuances beyond simply good or bad.

Attitudes influence people's choices, such as whether or not to take a risk, present an initiative, capture the spotlight, remain in the background, and more. They impact the actions that follow those choices. Attitudes dictate how people will respond to challenges – tackling them head on or running away. They frame people's responses to incentives and rewards.

Can an attitude run consistently across an entire organization, becoming part of its very culture? We believe so.

Values

Values form the internal DNA of an individual. A person's core values can serve as a compass, plumb line, or tuning fork for all his or her decisions in life. People who have identified their values have a road map to follow no matter what types of situations arise.

Values are highly personal, differing greatly from one person to the next. A simple look at the word "success" reveals this truth. Most people value success in some form, but their definitions of that word vary, and can involve finances, family dynamics, spiritual influence, or many other facets.

Do whole organizations possess values that run deep within their culture and guide the way they operate? No doubt.

There is nothing intrinsically good or bad about most values, but the behaviors that flow from them can be either. That's where the next characteristic of culture, morals, enters the conversation.

Morals

People have strongly-rooted beliefs that deem certain actions as fundamentally right or wrong. We refer to those as morals. While there are some basic agreements in society about the positive or negative morality of various behaviors, the lines have increasingly become blurred.

Morals can also be thought of as a code of conduct. They form the boundaries within which a person's values are lived out. Someone with a value of "financial prosperity" for example, may have an opportunity to further that value through means that are unethical. The decision of whether to pursue such an opportunity or not will depend upon the person's morals.

Organizations have morals as well, reflected in their Companality.

Work/Life Ethic

The level of effort and commitment which a person brings to his or her undertakings can be referred to as work ethic, or in a broader sense, life ethic. Some keep their nose to the grindstone, going far beyond the standard call of duty. Others are laid back and feel that good enough is good enough.

While neither of these extremes can be judged as better or worse, they are destined to produce very different outcomes. Taken to an organizational level, a particular work/life ethic will certainly be visible throughout the firm's culture.

The Characteristics Combined

Attitudes, values, morals, work/life ethic. In an individual, these characteristics are a large part of one's personality. In an organization, they are a major contributor to Companality.

Back to our definition of organizational culture, as we dive deeper into its next phrase:

... shared across an organization ...

Can it be that characteristics combine and form a culture across an entire organization? They certainly do. The proof is experienced thousands of times a day.

In fact, below is my own experience, which became the catalyst for my personal pursuit to understand this fascinating topic.

As the owner of an advertising agency for several decades, I worked with many different companies. There was one that, no matter what I was doing with them, made every encounter seem like a hassle. Whether it was a complex contract negotiation or just routine communication, there was always some problem or conflict.

Another company with which I did business was just the opposite. Their people were always pleasant, even when there was a complication or some challenge to overcome.

These experiences got me thinking about the predictability of my interactions with a variety of specific businesses. I realized that regardless of who I dealt with or what the matter was at hand, each had consistent characteristics.

It dawned on me that there had to be more than random occurrence behind it all; there had to be something within the fibers of these businesses that caused them to leave me with the exact same impressions every time we interacted.

Think about how consistent your interactions are with various organizations. Disney World and the driver's license renewal office are two strong cases in point. But what about McDonald's, Starbucks, the Post Office, Doubletree Hotels, Target, Subway? Whether it's the one near your home, on the other side of town, or across the country, a very predictable encounter awaits you. That doesn't happen by accident.

The examples don't stop with national chains. Consider that local restaurant, auto repair shop, hair salon, or insurance agency. No matter with which employee you interact – in person, electronically, or on the telephone – or what time of day or week, the experiences are amazingly alike. Why? Organizational culture.

Here again is our definition of organizational culture:

Organizational culture is
a combination of characteristics shared across an organization that dictate the experience of both customers and team

members as they interact with that organization.

We'll now discuss the next phrase.

... that dictate the experience of both customers and team members
...

Culture is also the determining factor in what it's like to work within an organization. The attitudes, values, morals, and work/life ethic of the organization in general certainly affect what it's like to show up in the morning and do one's job.

Like other elements of Companality, these factors are eerily similar throughout an office, store, shop, etc. And the consistencies go beyond single-location firms. So whether you're a team member at a Starbucks in Scranton, Pennsylvania or Scottsdale, Arizona, or a Target store in Fort Lee, New Jersey or Fort Myers, Florida, there's a commonality in the work environment.

Five people in one suite, or thousands of associates in multiple outlets worldwide. People who work for an organization largely share the same work experience. That's because the culture – the Companality – dictates this.

... as they interact with that organization ...

People engage with organizations in many ways. It starts with a telephone call, visit to a web site, or shopping encounter in a store. Then come conversations with receptionists, e-mail exchanges, and question and answer sessions. There may be prolonged negotiations. Relationships lasting years could be formed, or the whole transaction might be over within minutes.

Regardless of the contact between customer, patient, diner, client, patron (whatever they're called in a particular industry) and the businesses, restaurants, practices, non-profits or professions with which they interact, core organizational characteristics are revealed virtually every time. The reason for this is culture. Organizational culture.

Once more, the definition ...

Organizational culture is
a combination of characteristics shared across an organization that dictate the experience of both customers and team members as they interact with that organization.

And with a simple and logical substitution of the first words we have ...

Companality is
a combination of characteristics shared across an organization that dictate the experience of both customers and team members as they interact with that organization.

That's the meaning of Companality.

3

The Effects Of Companality

Companality dictates the type of interactions that people have with an organization. This determines the type of customers and employees the firm attracts, and eventually defines the organization's reputation.

Attracting The Right Customers

Humans identify with their brands. At first, people make purchase decisions only on necessity, utility, affordability, and similar criteria. As they mature as consumers, the selection of clothes, watches, cars, retail outlets, and more are based on alignment with a certain world view, politics, etc. The choices are designed to make statements of self expression.

Creating brand-loyal customers, therefore, requires more than offering a sterile transaction of going to a business and exchanging money for a product or service. Instead, customers want to feel a connection with the company and brand with which they identify. They want a meaningful experience throughout the entire experience, and far beyond – long after the sale has been made. They've joined a tribe, and they want to feel good about it.

This requires an intentional effort on the organization's part to craft and deliver a specific, unique experience in tune with the reason people chose that brand. And it must happen each and every time the firm and its customers interact. If not, the magic fades.

So in a very real sense, an organization's culture – Companality – affects the type of customer the enterprise attracts. Want to do business with high net worth individuals? Certainly you'll have to deliver a premium product or service, but you'll also have to deliver a premium customer experience along with it. And that only comes as the outgrowth of a premium culture.

Want people to respect your brand? Create a culture of respect. Looking for young, progressive nature lovers? Middle-aged, conservative, upwardly-mobile professionals? Your Companality will need to follow suit.

Yes, culture affects the type of consumer an organization attracts.

- Steve Shares -

You're A Customer. But I Must Say Goodbye.

Certain organizational cultures attract certain kinds of customers. If you want a specific customer type, intentionally develop a Companality that appeals to that category. So goes a Companality basic belief.

Sometimes, however, there's a glitch in the formula. A customer, client, patron, etc. slips in who is far from the desired profile. At that point things can get complicated.

No doubt you're in business to make money, so turning clients away should be a rarity. In my 30 years (as of this writing) of owning an advertising / marketing agency, I've only had to do it two or three times. What constitutes a situation where such drastic action is necessary? That's going to vary for every organization and its leadership.

Of course slow payers (or no payers) must be abandoned. But that's a no brainer and not a decision based on considerations of culture.

In my experience, the deed was done when clients displayed an extreme, unwarranted lack of respect for myself or members of the team, through no fault of our own. When we had truly done everything we knew to do to be humble servants, and the rhetoric was still on the negative side, it was time to part ways. I kept it professional and made it clear that the door was open for future possibilities.

I do my best not to look at any other human being as inherently bad. We've all got our good and not-so-good characteristics after all. It's possible that the same clients my company couldn't please found a mutually-beneficial professional relationship somewhere else, with an organization sporting a much different Companality.

For me, however, it was sad, but I had to say goodbye.

-- Author

Attracting The Right Employees

Internally, Companality establishes staff morale and is a leading factor in both the enthusiasm and productivity of the team. Associates will function a certain way and feel a certain way about their workplace based on the culture that exists there. Taken downstream, this will dictate the type of people who are attracted to join the firm.

A buttoned-down, highly corporate environment will be the workplace of choice for a different type of employee than a more laid-back office. Which staff member is most likely to be successful in your industry? Create the proper Companality and you'll attract those individuals.

Studies by top research firms reveal that the connection team members feel with their employers wield the greatest influence on the effort they put into their work. The major performance drivers are closely linked to the organization's Companality. Those include:

• Trust and integrity – How well managers communicate and then walk the talk are key builders of confidence and morale.

• Link between employee and company performance – Understanding how their work contributes to the organization's performance fosters a greater sense of responsibility and importance.

• Pride about the company – How much self-esteem does the employee feel by being associated with the company?

• Coworkers/team members – Positive camaraderie is essential in reducing turnover, improving motivation and boosting productivity. Relationships with coworkers significantly influence an employee's level of engagement.

• Relationship with managers – Does the employee feel comfortable, supported and encouraged in his or her relationship with a supervisor?

It's a simple fact. People prefer to work in organizations where the Companality matches their personal preferences. So think about the type of individuals you want on your team, and be sure that the organization's culture is one that will attract and retain them.

Creating The Right Reputation
Word gets around. So an organization's culture will also create its reputation within the marketplace in general. People will take notice of what the company stands for and how it's positioned among its competitors. Even those who may not do business with the company will become familiar with its reputation.

For example, someone who drives an economy vehicle is just as likely to have opinions about luxury car brands as the consumer who owns one. These influences, though indirect, have a profound effect on brand perception.

From employee-friendly national brands to local businesses that earn reputations as great places to work, company cultures that cultivate a highly supportive environment typically wind up with good outcomes. Likewise, when an organization loses its edge, or even closes its doors, it's often the result of a culture that was lacking in an important area.

– – – – –

Customers. Employees. Reputation. It's a cycle that's significantly affected by this thing called Companality. It's a major, make-or-break factor within any organization, and the fact that it often goes unrecognized makes it a resource of enormous untapped potential. Be sure to take advantage of this in your firm.

4

Meet Your Organizational Culture

Every organization – yours included – has a culture. Right now, that culture is influencing the entire enterprise, and will contribute significantly to success or failure. Whether you've ever acknowledged it or not, organizational culture is there, it's consistent, and it permeates your firm, affecting your customers, employees, reputation, and brand image.

Walk around the office. It's unlikely that one person's work station is overly messy while all the others are well organized. Observe the relative productivity of individuals. While there are always overachievers and underperformers, rarely do these dissimilar individuals exist side by side for long. From the way files are stored on the computer system to time spent at the water cooler, the level of sameness across an entire company is conspicuously high.

There are, of course, exceptions. In these scenarios it's every person for him or her self, creating cultures of anarchy. But even anarchy is consistent when everyone in the organization lives only for number one. And these entities flame out prematurely in just that way.

Make no mistake, your organization has a Companality. Was it developed intentionally by the leadership of the company, or did it come about in some other way? That's a question worth serious consideration.

Let's go there.

5

Where Does Organizational Culture Originate?

The premise of the Companality concept is that it is possible for the leaders of an organization to develop the entity's culture intentionally, through a defined process. But without conscious efforts to build culture, other factors take over and set the course. A culture is created, for sure, however it is anything but intentional.

Let's look at a few of the factors that might form a culture far afield of the desires of upper management.

Variations Within Your Industry
The very industry in which a company exists has a large effect on its culture. A law firm will be fundamentally different from a music recording studio or a surf shop. Dress codes, hours of

operation, accepted vocabulary, management styles and more may bear no resemblance to one another across diverse types of organizations.

A company's industry is an established fact, so there is little that management can do about this factor of the culture's origin. It is best to accept this and not fight too aggressively against it, though some latitude does exist.

Careful consideration should be given to the factors that vary from one company to the next within an industry. That's where the intentional development of the Companality becomes so important.

In one law practice, the attorneys are treated like royalty, with covered parking spaces, catered lunches, a special wash room, and more – while the support staff enjoys none of those amenities. The firm down the street treats everyone equally in those respects, regardless of the letters after their names. No doubt similarities exist, across thier industry. But the Companality differences are noteworthy.

Auto mechanic A believes in a pristine environment, shiny tools, neat uniforms, and the latest technology. Shop B takes it old school, earning the down and dirty "grease monkey" connotation.

In both the above examples, we see that a variation of cultures can exist within the same industry. And if these are not developed intentionally, they've happened some other way.

Strong-Willed Staff Members

In the absence of a culture that is being established intentionally, employees often fill the gap. The most outspoken and bold among them will bring their own preferences to the organization. Other employees follow suit, and a culture is firmly in place.

The conduct can be overt or covert. Both, sadly, are effective – often to the detriment of the culture.

An employee with a negative attitude, values that are expressed through questionable morals, and a less than stellar work/life ethic is likely to go from work station to work station spreading complaints and discontent. When this behavior is unchecked, or even worse, unnoticed, the sentiments catch on. It doesn't take long for the whole culture to be affected.

Strong-willed staff members who frame the culture often find ways to subtly punish employees who try to set the bar higher. Snide comments, exclusion from the inner circle, ridiculing, and other bullying techniques can cause a good employee to fall in line at a lower performance level, or – more likely – resign from the firm.

In these and other ways, staff members themselves can set the culture. This is often not healthy for the company.

What Management Allows

Organizational culture comes about by default when management sets rules that aren't enforced. The leaders say "here at XYZ Corp, we do it this way" or "we never allow this behavior," but the actual culture is determined as a result of what people get away with.

The employee manual states a mandatory start time for the work day. But someone comes in ten minutes late several mornings in a row, and his or her supervisor says nothing. Others notice and become less concerned about what time they arrive to work. This can lead to a culture where schedules, breaks, and even deadlines are not given a high degree of respect regardless of what upper management believes to be the case.

A beautiful poster, created by a graphic design firm and approved by the CEO states "Our Associates Treat Customers Like Royalty." Walking by a row of cubicles, however, a supervisor hears two employees talking negatively about a long-time client who called about an error in a recent shipment. The supervisor casts a glance at one of the employees, catching his eye, but says nothing and keeps walking.

It's a trite expression that actions speak louder than words. The truth of that phrase, however, can not be ignored when it comes to the development of organizational culture. The team is paying attention to management's actions as much or more than listening to what is said. If the actions indicate that a certain cultural attitude is or is not allowed, that action will become an element of the culture.

We've Always Done It This Way

Status quo cultures are dangerous. These occur when leaders within an organization become enlightened to the importance of intentionally developing a Companality and try to turn the ship, only to encounter resistance.

The push back from employees is rarely based on mal intent, but instead may very well come from a belief that the way things are handled currently is just fine. To combat this, leadership must paint a picture of a brighter future, detailing how the new environment will include cultural improvements.

Change is tough. Challenges to it are often not blatant, but more of a subtle tendency to continue to think and act in ways that were always accepted in the past. Constant observation is required to root out these trends, and then skillfully reinforce the innovations that management believes are in line with a more beneficial culture.

- Steve Shares -

Is Unintentional Always Bad?

Every company has a Companality, and many of them are developed through some means other than the intentional efforts of management. Does it always turn out bad? Well no.

I freely acknowledge that not every organizational culture that has emerged without the benefit of the processes written in these pages is devastatingly horrible. In fact, most company's cultures have been built just that way, and in many cases the results are satisfactory.

But we don't know what we don't know. So I wonder what those organizations could be like with some focused activities brought to bear on this important aspect of business.

It therefore remains my assertion and the premise of this book that cultures which are not intentionally developed are very often less than ideal. And those which do follow certain steps will come to enjoy all the benefits that a well-conceived, desired Companality brings.

-- Author

Only through embracing a deliberate process of cultural renovation can the reluctance to abandon old norms be overcome.

It's important for management to understand that the current culture, if not developed intentionally, was created through some other means. It may be a reflection of an aspect of the organization's industry, or the course set by strong-willed employees. The culture may have come about via the signals sent by what management has allowed, because of an aversion to change the way things were always done in the past, or as a result of other factors. And the culture will continue to evolve according to arbitrary influences, unless they, the leaders, get involved.

Many organizational leaders and founders have admirable philosophies about life and business. Positive attitudes. Lofty values. Morals rooted in integrity. Strong work ethics. Too often, they believe that these characteristics will automatically transfer to the organizations they launched or manage. They expect a like-minded Companality in keeping with their own personalities. Certain characteristics are second nature to them, so the organization's culture will follow suit, they think.

That's a grave mistake.

The creation of a specific culture does not happen by default. It can only be developed through specific, intentional efforts.

6

Taking Control
With Companality

The good news is that it is possible to intentionally develop an organization's culture, or Companality. Broadly speaking, the method for doing so is found right in that statement, in the words "intentionally develop." It must be developed, and the process must be intentional. Let's look at those two words one at a time.

Intentionally

Effective organizational cultures are the result of intentional efforts. There are specific steps that an organization must follow, and techniques to apply in order to achieve a distinct culture. Cultures that happen without the benefit of intentional efforts rarely stand out. Only by taking pre-defined, proven steps in a pre-meditated, conscious way will organizations achieve the

Companality they want.

Develop

Intentional corporate culture develops over time. This is a process. Building the culture initially, or changing a current undesirable Companality, will be like constructing a skyscraper, with each floor supported by the one beneath it.

– – – – –

It is common for management to try and change culture overnight, thinking that a mandatory meeting and a few motivational posters will usher in new attitudes throughout the firm. This expectation is sure to fail. Instead, it's vitally important to realize from the start that developing an effective Companality is a long-range project, and one which must be tackled with specific goals and a plan. In other words, intentionally.

Fortunately, there's a process for this and tools to help make it happen.

7

Companality
And Purpose

As we've seen so far, organizational culture affects a firm in at least three ways: attracting the right customers, attracting the right employees, and defining the firm's reputation. It's also been stated that it is possible for an organization to develop its culture intentionally. We're about to explore a process and tools for doing that.

Purpose Statements

The first step is to pause and consider something that's at the very core of the entity's culture. This could be the most foundational culture development exercise the organization can undertake. It's done by asking and answering the following question:

"What is this organization's purpose?"

Imagine any type of commercial entity. (Non-profits have their own idiosyncrasies, which we'll see later.) Insurance agency, residential real estate brokerage, funeral parlor, accounting firm, dental office, bicycle shop, jewelry store, and the organization where you work or that you lead today.

What is that organization's purpose?

It might seem that the simple answer for a business is "To make money." Woe, however, to the business that does answer the question solely that way. While it might make sense in the short term, over time the entity is doomed to a culture of adversarial relationships among team members and with customers, leading to a disastrous reputation.

Every organization will have its unique culture. But it's safe to say that organizations which attract the most valuable customers and build stellar reputations have teams comprising people drawn to loftier purposes. Making a sole owner, a group of shareholders – or even themselves – wealthy simply isn't enough.

Is there a specific purpose that always inspires the right culture? Not exactly. It is very likely that quality employees will be most enthusiastic about a purpose that reflects some tangible benefit to those the organization serves, but even that is not a hard and fast rule. In truth, each entity will have to answer the question "What is this organization's purpose?" for itself. And the more team members that can be involved in crafting that answer, the better, as the final outcome will have enormous ramifications.

The goal should be to brainstorm, discuss, draft and re-draft, finally ending at a written purpose statement that is brief, memorable, and simple to understand. Further, the purpose statement must be applicable across every part of the organization: front desk, sales, administration, marketing, human resources, production, finance – you name it. It must tug on the emotions of all involved, going beyond mere intellectual ascent to that part of each team member that inspires a true connection with the organization's mission.

Considering a few types of organizations from the earlier list, here are examples of potential purpose statements. As you'll see, there is a great deal of latitude in how such a statement might be written:

Insurance Agency – Long version – *We protect people's lifestyles from financial loss and disruptions by providing insurance policies that meet their needs. And we do so using simple, uncomplicated language that is easy for our customers to understand.*

Insurance Agency – Short version – *We protect people's lifestyles.*

Residential Real Estate Brokerage – Option 1 – *We fulfill people's dreams.*

Residential Real Estate Brokerage – Option 2 – *We help people find and obtain their dream homes, taking care to ensure that they stay within their budgets, so that they can enjoy those homes for years to come.*

Bicycle Shop – *We offer advice, products, and services that enable people to lead healthier lifestyles, and find great enjoyment in the process.*

It should be noted that these purpose statements all express how their organizations benefit people. While not a cardinal rule, as mentioned above, such statements generally resonate most clearly with the types of team members who build effective organizational cultures, attract appreciative customers, and create positive corporate reputations.

A Word About Non-Profit Purpose Statements

When it comes to crafting a purpose statement, non-profits pose unique challenges.

Think about a conventional, for-profit business. In most cases, the people supporting the company and the people using the company's services are one and the same. A patron gives a coffee shop money and gets a cup of coffee in return. A customer writes a check to a car dealership and drives away in a new car.

Non-profits and charities are different from for-profits in that respect. For a non-profit, the people receiving the service are generally separate from the people who lay out the financial support that makes the service possible. Homeless men and women may receive meals and a place to sleep from a non-profit organization, but the funds that make those meals and shelter possible will have come from an entirely different set of people.

As the leaders of a non-profit entity embark upon defining the organization's purpose, the needs and interests of both the clients: those receiving services; and the donors: those providing the money; must be considered.

For the homeless food kitchen and shelter, for example, a purpose statement might be something like – *We bring appealing, delicious meals, and clean, safe overnight housing to the homeless men and women in our community, while providing donors with the opportunity to make a difference in the lives of these homeless individuals and know that they are deeply appreciated for doing so.*

This sample non-profit purpose statement is just a single example of one that covers all the bases. A similar mentality and dual thinking will affect other aspects of the Companality process for non-profits as well.

— — — — —

Whether for-profit or non-profit, an organization in any industry and of any size must, as part of the foundation of its culture, identify its reason for existence. The reason should evoke emotion in everyone who works on and within that culture and, ideally, contain an element describing how the organization benefits a bigger picture. The route to get there is by asking and answering the question, "What is this organization's purpose?"

8

Preparing For
The Journey

Before taking the next step in the Companality process, it will help to briefly review several premises that have been presented thus far. Broadly stated, they are:

• Every organization has a culture, also known as Companality.

• Companality is fundamentally a reflection of the attitudes, values, morals, and work/life ethic of the people within the organization and of the organization itself.

• Companality has major effects on many aspects of an organization, most notably the clientele it attracts, the types of people who want to be its employees, and its reputation in the marketplace.

• If an organization's culture was not developed intentionally, according to the leadership's desires, it was probably developed by factors which are often undesirable.

• It IS possible to intentionally develop an organization's culture.

• The first step is to define the organization's purpose.

– – – – –

It's now time to paint a clear picture of how a finished Companality will look in your specific organization.

9

The Companality Vision

In order to reach a destination, you have to know where you're going. That's equally true for a leadership team that wishes to intentionally develop its organization's culture. A clear picture of how the Companality should look, feel, and be implemented in practice is key to the project's success.

Our next goal, therefore, is to create what can be called the Companality Vision. Once this vision is firmly in place, the firm's higher-ups can begin the intentional, step-by-step approach outlined later in this book to get there. As the business matures, the vision will be the benchmark against which operations are subordinated. All future decisions will have to pass the test of whether or not they support this vision.

Crafting a Companality Vision should be a fun, fluid exercise, restricted by only a few factors. Most importantly the vision must be in line with the organization's purpose, captured in a defined purpose statement, as discussed in a previous chapter. Legal and ethical boundaries must be respected of course. And it must be an accurate depiction of what the leaders deem will best serve their industry, clients and team members.

Beyond those factors, there is nothing inherently right or wrong about a Companality Vision and the culture it will eventually guide. That's not to say that every culture results in business success. Consumers, voting with their patronage, will determine that downstream. But it does mean that when brainstorming the culture's course, nothing should be off the table.

– – – – –

The most valuable resource for creating a Companality Vision is a resource known as the Companality Continuum. We'll now explore how the Companality Continuum works.

10

The
Companality
Continuum

The best way to depict the concept of creating a Companality Vision may be via the use of a continuum. A continuum starts with a simple line, like this:

Topic Here

One Extreme--Other Extreme

On the far left of the line is a style of a behavior. On the far right is the opposite style of the same behavior. Of course there are many possibilities between the two ends of the continuum.

For example, if the continuum line were charting the goals of runners who compete in road races, the left extreme might represent a very slow pace where the right extreme would represent a very fast pace. Individual runners could chart their own goals somewhere on the line, slower runners more toward the left, faster runners more toward the right.

Managers and leaders can use such a tool for the visioning of organizational culture. We call this the Companality Continuum. On the Companality Continuum, management will plot various elements of the professional world, then determine where their desired organizational culture best fits on the continuum.

During this step there are no specific right or wrong responses. That will be determined far down the line by the success or failure of the organization. The importance of the current exercise is for managers to simply clarify their vision of what they want the Companality of the organization to be at some point in the future.

Leadership

Let's start with leadership, and explore how it might be incorporated into an organization's Companality Vision, using the Companality Continuum. We'll start with a simple continuum line, labeled "Leadership."

Leadership

Looking at both ends of the continuum, an organization can be either leader directed, or individual directed. The Companality Continuum, as it pertains to leadership, therefore, would look like this:

Leadership

Leader Directed----------------------------------Individual Directed

An organizational culture functioning on the far left side of this line would be completely leader directed. Taken to the extreme, which the far side of a continuum indicates, the bosses in this culture would tell subordinates exactly what to do and when, where and how to do it. These bosses may or may not share the "why", as this culture might not feel it's important for employees to know why, but that they should simply do as they're told.

The far right side of the Leadership portion of the Companality Continuum represents a culture that is totally individual directed. In this organization, people are expected to uncover what needs to be done, within or maybe even outside their sphere of responsibility, and then do it. The boss, to the extent he or she can be identified, is just one of the players, with perhaps an enhanced ability to provide experience, insight and resources. He or she helps facilitate the individuals as they embark upon projects and tasks.

Between these two extremes on the continuum there are nearly infinite ways that an organization can define the leadership elements of its culture. Some will be more toward the leader directed side of the line, and some more toward the individual directed side.

And remember, there is no right or wrong during this exercise. Management must simply define what it wants its Companality to be in this area of leadership.

We'll follow the same process with other aspects of organizational culture.

Motivational Method

Managers who disregard consensus and place little value in positive reinforcement of their employees don't win popularity contests. But they can be effective. Case in point: the late Apple leader Steve Jobs. Known for his demanding nature and blunt delivery of criticism, Jobs' visionary skills and insistence on greatness gave staff, investors and customers a rise to the top. If you picture a culture of strict accountability for results as the supreme objective, this method of motivation, on the left end of the continuum, may be for you.

At the other end of the Companality Continuum is the more empowering, employee-centric method. Here, supervisors who consistently extend respect, trust, and encouragement to their teams can send motivation levels soaring. These managers relate effectively with employees, show that they are personally interested in and care about them, and elicit input and opinions. Two distinct motivational methods, with many options represented by points all along the continuum, all capable of producing results. The one that best suits the vision you have for achieving your mission will play a key part in shaping your organization's Companality.

Motivational Method

Demanding---Empowering

How Decisions Are Made

Top down decision-making cultures leave no question about who has the authority. Others may be in charge of certain areas of the organization's operations, but somebody higher up is always in the loop and makes the final call.

The front lines approach on the other end of the continuum exists when employees are entrusted to make decisions consistent with their areas of expertise and levels of responsibility, so long as they feel comfortable to do so.

Even on the front lines end of the Companality Continuum, there is often another "boss" that supports the decision-making process: the organizational chart. Consulting a clear, simple org chart can provide the security of knowing exactly where to go for advice, assistance, a sounding board, or confirmation of a possible direction.

Who makes decisions? It could be a few select people at the top (left side), a much larger number of those on the front lines (right side), or a hybrid style somewhere in between. Either way, it's a Companality choice that will greatly affect your organization's ability to get things done and stay on a course in line with your desired culture.

How Decisions Are Made

Top Down--Front Lines

Tackling Tasks

How an organization approaches the way tasks are carried out is another element that must be plotted on the Companality Continuum. In a traditional, hierarchical organizational structure, managers hand work down to people who directly report to them, and the work is then done by the assigned employee.

In a more team-oriented approach, employees are encouraged to take on tasks when they notice issues or opportunities. They may even have the freedom to proactively collaborate with their co-workers to address those tasks or larger projects. Most organizations will find their vision somewhere in between the two ends. The continuum line for this element is shown below.

Tackling Tasks

Work Alone And Report Upward-----------------Team Approach

Work Space

There are varying ideas about what constitutes the perfect work space. Some organizations prefer private offices where each person can operate in seclusion. Other firms opt for open areas without walls of any kind, in order to form a collaborative environment. Often, it's a mix of both. What's right for one company may not be right for another. The critical part is that management have a vision for how this element fits into its own Companality.

Work Space

Private Offices----------------------------------Open Environment

Schedules

The 9 to 5, five days a week American work schedule isn't as typical as it used to be. Accommodating a flextime work-life balance can be a key factor in recruiting and retaining good employees who often respond to the privilege with greater productivity and dedication. Or for some businesses, it can be problematic to coordinate people, tasks and productivity when employees aren't at work at the same place at the same time, at least on some regular basis.

Wherever your organization falls on the continuum of flexible work schedules, be aware of its significance as a Companality benchmark.

Schedules

Strict Office Hours--Flex Time

Dress Code

An organization's dress code contributes to its Companality in several ways. It can create a mindset within individual employees, establish an atmosphere of camaraderie and uniformity, set the tone for how customers perceive the organization, and give team members a range of expression. Ideally, each of these results should fit within the company's identity and standards. Whether formal, casual, or somewhere in between on the Companality Continuum, dress codes certainly form part of a company's culture.

Dress Code

Business Formal--Casual

Orderliness

Some people thrive on chaos. Their desks and offices are stacked high with papers, and their computer file systems are the digital equivalent. In short, anything goes.

Others require neatness, with a place for everything and everything in its place. The principle of Companality says that there will be fairly even consistency throughout the enterprise. How much orderliness is the right amount? That depends on the type of Companality a specific company's management wants.

The many alternatives can be plotted on a continuum line like the one below.

Orderliness

A Place For Everything------------------------------Anything Goes

Ambient Noise

Noise can be a valid part of some work environments – dance clubs, sports bars, and the floor of the New York Stock Exchange to name a few. Lively, spirited people exchanging their thoughts isn't necessarily a bad thing. But if your organization depends on concentrated focus and thoughtful communication to get work done, a constant clamor can be detrimental.

Better lend an ear to that wise voice in your head that knows how much direct and ambient noise is the right amount to feed or foil the Companality you seek. Whatever you decide, there's a place on the Companality Continuum for it.

Ambient Noise

Silence Is Golden----------------------------Noise Is No Problem

And More

Since no two organizations are the same, there can be many additional elements to plot on the Companality Continuum. Each one will affect the culture that management wishes to create. Whether it's community involvement, professional development, office décor, rewards and recognition, or one of numerous other puzzle pieces, leaders must create Companality Continuum lines depicting the alternatives. They must then carefully plot the point on the continuum that most resembles their Companality Vision for that factor.

Once again, here's how the continuum process works. Use it for the variables listed above, or any factors that uniquely pertain to your industry and firm.

Topic Here

One Extreme--Other Extreme

There's no rush, so give the visioning process plenty of time and attention. When it comes to Companality, clarity counts.

- *Steve Shares* -

A Tale Of Two Meatballs

Here's a story from my own personal experience that describes a Companality utilizing a Top Down approach to How Decisions Are Made, vs. a more Front Lines mentality. This employee seems to have had zero authority to do something even a little out of the ordinary, no matter how logical. Or if he did, that fact hadn't been communicated to him.

It was one of those long days that business travelers know well. After hours spent in airports, on planes, and driving a rental car, I was finally in my hotel room. I just wanted to order food, iron a shirt, and handle my e-mail while eating dinner.

As usual, the choices for food delivery – aside from room service which wasn't in the budget – were Chinese and Italian. Italian got the nod. The menu was limited: pizza, which I try not to eat more than rarely, and spaghetti and meatball. Decision made.

The telephone conversation went something like this ...

Restaurant Person (RP): _____ _____ *Pizzeria. How may I help you?*

Me: *I'd like to order spaghetti and meatball for delivery.*

He takes my address etc.

RP: *Today is buy one get one day. Would you like a second meal for free?*

Me: *Wow, that's great! But it's just me here and I won't eat two complete meals, so just give me an extra meatball.*

RP: *No problem. That's $11.99 for the meal and two dollars for the extra meatball.*

Me: *I'm sorry. Maybe I wasn't clear. Instead of taking a whole meal of spaghetti and meatball for free, I'll just take an extra meatball for free.*

RP: *Yes, Sir. I understand. But I have no way of doing that.*

Me: *All you have to do is add a meatball to my order of spaghetti and meatball.*

RP: *I have no way of doing that.*

Me: *How about this? Make two meals of spaghetti and meatball. Take the meatball out of one meal and put it in the other. Send the meal with two meatballs to me, then give the other meal to someone or eat it yourself.*

RP: *Sir, I totally get what you want, but I have no way of doing that.*

Me: *Fine. I'll pay the extra two dollars.*

And that was that.

-- Author

11

Companality
Day To Day

Effective culture comes about only through intentional long-range efforts within a defined methodology. Developing a Companality that supports the organization's purpose statement and is in keeping with the Companality Vision requires the successful implementation of specific techniques that become part of the everyday routine of the company. These include:

Staff Accordingly
Get Buy In
Train
Communicate
Model
Reward & Counsel
Be Consistent

Let's look at these individually.

Staff Accordingly

People are the critical element in an organization. It only takes a credit card to rent office space, buy desks and computers, obtain supplies, have telephones installed, and print business cards. But equipment and facilities alone do not create culture.

Many business leaders think that if they simply hire "good people," those staff members can later be molded into adherents of the organization's desired culture. This is a big mistake and will often result in frustration for both management and employee. Instead, an organization must have its Companality in mind from the very beginning of the recruiting process and throughout it, right up until the new hire comes on board.

Intentionally developing organizational culture by staffing accordingly starts with the candidate recruitment posting. Consider the two posts below. Both seek an Executive Assistant for an advertising agency, but the type of person to which these announcements appeal will vary greatly.

Recruitment Post # 1 ...

Ad Agency Seeks Executive Assistant
The Executive Assistant will provide support for the agency president through daily management of agency activities, as

well as serve as the liaison between external and internal contacts when appropriate.

The Executive Assistant must be well organized, detail oriented, and able to perform job responsibilities that include:
- Calendar management
- Meeting scheduling
- Organizing travel
- Expense reporting
- Email and other correspondence
- Answering phones
- Presentation preparation
- Business related errands

Job Skills & Requirements:
- 10+ years as an Administrative Assistant; 5+ years supporting senior management
- Bachelor's degree
- Strong computer skills
- Strong oral/written communication, organization, and interpersonal skills
- Professional and positive attitude

Now take a look at a recruitment post for the same position in a dramatically different organizational culture.

Recruitment Post #2 …

Wanted: Executive Assistant With A Creative Soul
A high-energy, creative-worshipping ad agency is seeking an
impact player for the position of Executive Assistant to the
President. Are you a self-starter who can manage who-knows-
how-many tasks, thrive in a fast-paced environment and laugh
in the face of competing priorities? Are you a fresh thinker with
a fertile mind who isn't shy about jumping in with a new idea
– even if it's "not your job"?

Sure, we need someone who is professional, organized and
dependable; someone who can manage the boss's calendar,
schedule meetings and make travel arrangements; someone with
a relevant college education and who's seen it all and done it all
before. But we also need someone who can brainstorm, express
an idea or opinion, and bring a spark to a team that uses sparks
to light the next creative fire.

As you can see, these recruiting efforts are likely to appeal to and
generate excitement in two distinct types of people. And that's
good, as the goal is to staff with the Companality in mind from
the very beginning. Neither is right, wrong, good, bad, or better
than the other. They simply reflect varying cultures.

Once a candidate has been introduced to the organization's
culture in this way, it is important to provide reinforcement.
The person doing the interview should introduce the candidate

to the firm's purpose statement and relevant elements of the Companality Vision. Examples should be given of how the firm's culture affects daily operations.

These company / candidate interactions are a two-way street. Whatever the hiring process, it should include several opportunities for both sides to make an informed, enlightened decision, not only about job duties, salary and all the other elements of personnel selection, but also about the culture. The candidate must be given a clear understanding of the Companality within which he or she might be working in the future. And the company needs clarity as to whether or not this person will be a cultural fit.

The gut feeling known as "chemistry" is too important to overlook. Violating this will almost always result in a hire that is not aligned with the organization's culture. Down the road, this will either chip away at the firm's culture or result in an unhappy team member and supervisor. The person will likely leave the organization before long, either voluntarily or otherwise. Given the cost of recruiting, hiring, and training personnel, this can be devastating to the enterprise.

The Companality Continuum – the visioning process at the heart of organizational culture to which you were introduced earlier in this book – can become an even more valuable aid during this process. You've done the hard work of plotting your vision of various aspects of the culture you wish to create, so you can use it to pose questions designed to reveal a job candidate's compatibility with this culture.

For example, you might ask "How do you like to work? Do you prefer silence, or do you like some conversation or music? Do you like strict office hours or flex time? Are you more productive in your own private office or are you better suited to an open, team environment?" While conversational on the surface, the answers to these and other questions will help identify someone who does or does not match the vision you've previously defined using the Companality Continuum.

Developing a pre-hire form for interviewers with corresponding notes highlighting each question's purpose can be another valuable culture-driven staffing tool.

The following sample reflects an organization whose Companality Vision includes the elements of customer service, building customer loyalty, internal collaboration, initiative, and integrity. The prepared questions are designed to dig deeper into a job candidate's compatibility with such a culture.

Company Culture Related Questions
for the Pre-Hire Interview

Interviewer Intro to Candidate: *Our company culture is a vital part of how we connect with our customers and each other. I'm going to ask you some questions related to our culture here and would like to get your thoughts.*

1) How do you go about building positive relationships with customers? Can you share an example from your experience?

Interviewer Note: We're looking for evidence that the candidate has excellent people skills and knows how to make customers feel understood, important and appreciated.

2) Tell me about a time at work when you had an especially fulfilling or satisfying experience.

Interviewer Note: We're looking to see if the candidate makes a connection between job satisfaction and creating an exceptional customer experience.

3) Some professionals like to take the ball and run with it, and some like to tackle tasks in collaboration with coworkers. Tell us about your preferred style of working.

Interviewer Note: We're looking for the candidate's experience and comfort level in a team-oriented culture that thrives on collaboration.

4) What do you view as the keys to success in performing your job at a high level?

Interviewer Note: We're looking to see if the candidate

has a set of standards that guide his or her approach to excelling in a job. Ideally, those standards will be compatible with our culture, including elements such as teamwork, customer service, customer loyalty, initiative, and integrity.

5) What do you feel are the little things that have a big impact on how customers feel about a company?

Interviewer Note: We're looking to gauge a candidate's awareness of the attitudes and actions that make a big impact on great customer service and earn customer loyalty. Examples include listening, smiling, prompt response, following up on an issue or concern, showing appreciation, etc.

6) What qualities or traits would you say best reflect your personality and values?

Interviewer Note: Along with professional aptitude, we're looking to evaluate a candidate's personal makeup and potential to embody core qualities that align with our purpose statement.

7) Tell me about a time when you added value by going beyond the basic requirements of a job?

Interviewer Note: We're looking for examples of a candidate's ability to be proactive, take initiative, and find opportunities to improve on standard performance criteria.

8) Tell me about something unusual or creative you did to wow a customer.

Interviewer Note: We're looking for examples of out-of-the-box thinking to impress customers and earn their loyalty and advocacy.

9) Tell me about a time when you went above and beyond to help a co-worker.

Interviewer Note: We're looking to see if the candidate is a team player with a willingness to shift priorities and pitch in when a co-worker needs assistance.

When a strong fit leads to an offer of employment, the time is ripe to underscore the importance of organizational culture once again. Telling new hires that what set them apart from the many other skilled applicants was their cultural synergy sends a big message at a pivotal time.

Management's goal during the hiring process must be that candidates get a strong impression that the organization has a distinct culture and that the culture deliberately affects the actual nuts and bolts, day to day inner workings of the firm, including the type of people who are invited to become team members. The new hire's reaction should be "Wow, they're really serious about this culture thing!"

Get Buy-In

Organizations with intentionally developed Companality get buy-in from employees at every level. When everyone in the organization is made to feel that they are a contributing part of the culture, they take ownership of the culture's values and goals. Then, instead of organizational culture being something imposed by an outside force, it resides inside them as part of who they are and how they do their jobs.

Building a team that buys into the culture 100% requires puposeful, daily efforts. It's a process, not a one-time meeting at a conference center or special event. People may walk away from a corporate rally with a sense of hype, but that fades quickly. Buy-in that's developed with diligence is much more likely to stick.

The main ingredient of this process is dialogue. Management must continually solicit input, listen carefully to the feedback, ask questions for clarification, and enter honest discussions. What's more, every member of the team must feel that he or she has the freedom to weigh in on the culture at any time.

The organization's purpose statement and Companality Vision will be critical elements in these talks, as thoughts and opinions are evaluated by these benchmarks to see if they stand up. When an employee at any level of the firm has an idea or initiative that modifies the culture more clearly toward the purpose statement or vision, that element of the culture should be altered accordingly and with deep appreciation. While this might be a hit to the ego of someone higher on the organizational chart, the effect on team buy-in to the culture will be enormous.

At times, more sweeping adjustments to the culture may become necessary and appropriate, based on changes in the very direction or vision of the organization. If ever there is a Companality change of such significance, getting buy-in is even more critical. Team members must feel that they still own the culture and play a significant role in keeping it. The methodology in such instances will be the same as before: Dialogue.

Train

New employees need to go through a training process that puts learning the culture on par with the many other onboarding topics of starting a new job. Just as important as procedures for requesting vacation time, computer usage, where to find the key to the wash room, etc., are elements of the Companality Vision.

This training comes in several forms. It will typically be conducted by management of course, but it is even more effective for at least parts of the training to be handled by co-workers who embody the culture in admirable ways. These rank and file quality examples of the culture can be recognized as Companality Ambassadors, Companality Champions, or some other relevant title.

Formal cultural awareness meetings can take place where the trainers stand in front of a room and deliver prepared presentations. The content will center on how the culture is lived out day to day.

Culture can also be the topic of informal sessions involving both new and long-term staff. Supervisors as well as Companality Ambassadors/Champions should always be on the lookout for opportunities to share examples of how the culture plays out, and the related benefits. These can occur at any time such as while meeting in the hall, pouring a cup of coffee, or walking to the parking lot.

In addition to designated ambassadors, all the veterans of the organization's mindset should have their eyes open to ways they can help new co-workers. These interactions will ideally be happening constantly, everywhere in the office, shop, or store. Just a few minutes here and there from someone who's lived the culture for several years will send a strong message to the recently hired team member.

Communicate

The role that communication plays in reinforcing a desired culture cannot be overstated. It's doubtful that any employee has ever complained that the organization in which he or she works communicates too much. Sadly, the opposite complaint, "There's not enough communication here", is nearly universal in companies that are not intentional about this essential element of developing culture.

Within the parameters of a specific Companality Vision as plotted on the Companality Continuum, the basic guidelines for communication are simple:

What gets communicated? Just as much as possible.
To whom? Everyone.
When? All the time.
How? Through every available means.

In an effective Companality, there is virtually no such thing as insignificant information or operating on a need to know basis. In fact, letting people gain awareness and understanding of items that fall outside their direct areas of responsibility gives them a sense of belonging and even greater ownership of the culture. Certainly, some matters (sensitive financial and payroll information, for instance) are confidential, and there are times when information should not be relayed until final decisions of situations in progress are made, but generally a posture of liberal communication has only positive results.

Too many organizations share their vision of culture solely with top management. This overlooks the obvious truth that for a Companality to be valid, it must permeate the entire organization at every level.

Leaders often assume that others have an innate understanding of the general principles that guide how the firm operates. "It's second nature to me, so why not to them?" they think. But organizational culture does not trickle down magically. It must be developed through intentional communication that extends to every person on the team.

The same applies to the specifics of culture. Items as granular as dress code, as procedural as how the phones are answered, and as high-level as the philosophy of showing respect to vendors must be stated specifically and often. The Companality Vision may dictate that proper grammar, even in e-mails and text messages, is key, but if that is not communicated to everyone in the organization, the actual day to day operation may not reflect this value.

Communication cannot be hit and miss. Opportunities to underscore the culture are everywhere, and each one must be utilized. This could include formal proclamations such as the official purpose statement poster on the wall, the employee handbook, and other corporate materials. More casual methods such as regular e-mails, memos, blog postings, etc. should also be utilized. An organization-wide Intranet, on which team members can share feedback, provides a two-way forum of expression that can be especially valuable. The possibilities for communication are endless.

Companality can be expressed in subtle communications as well, by announcing employees' achievements on or off the job. Highlighting that someone in the bookkeeping department completed a marathon, for example, underscores the organization's appreciation of fitness, discipline, and accomplishing goals. Similarly, sharing company milestones with the entire team reinforces a sense of forward motion and the firm's belief in having a positive outlook. The messages go far deeper than just the information itself.

Through ongoing communication, the values, attitudes, morals, and work/life ethic of the organization will be kept in the forefront, perpetuating the Companality that supports it.

- Steve Shares -

The TMI Roller Coaster

I wish I had a dollar for every time a client told me he or she was going to give my company so much business that we'd soon be on the Fortune 100 list. Or how about fifty cents for every night's sleep lost to worrying about some looming disaster? Anyone who owns a business or runs a profit center can relate. But of course rarely do mountainous highs or crushing lows come to pass, at least not to a life-changing degree.

One of the tenets of Companality is that the right amount of information to share with the team is pretty much everything. So what falls into the gap between 100% and something less? What's appropriate and what's Too Much Information? Each organization's leadership is going to have to answer those questions for themselves.

Personally, I've never felt it prudent to get employees overly excited about a one in a million possibility. I might mention that "there are some big opportunities in the works," but going into detail doesn't seem like a good idea. History says there's a good chance I'd have to backtrack in the future.

Likewise, sowing depression in the workplace, or worse: giving people a reason to think about jumping ship isn't my thing. Very likely the storm will pass.

If the deal gets signed or the big client goes elsewhere, then certainly a celebration or rallying of the troops is in order. That's communication. When these things are not at all certain, however – well, that might be another story.

My title and position on the organizational chart carry with them the unpleasant requirement of a ride on the emotional roller coaster. I've made an intentional decision, for better or worse, not to pass that along.

What about you? How do you plan to navigate these waters in your own Companality?

-- Author

Model

People follow what they see much more than what they are told. To maintain a culture in line with the organization's vision, therefore, everyone responsible for promoting that culture must walk the talk. Leaders who do so are enormously valuable to the culture. Those who do otherwise must not be tolerated.

When it comes to adhering to culture, personnel at the top, including occupants of the C suite, managers, supervisors, directors, and any Companality Ambassadors and Champions will need to be toughest on themselves. The rest of the team is watching. Closely. Any indication that someone more senior in the organization is an exception will be taken as a sign that the elements of culture are optional.

Although the relationship may not be official or openly stated, employees view their bosses as mentors, and aspire to be like them in many aspects of the job. This is obvious in terms of skills, experience, respect, salary, etc. In an environment where culture is highly valued, team members will also look up to their supervisors when observing ways to live out that culture day by day. The actions of those higher up set a standard which their direct reports will want to meet in order to please their bosses. When those actions involve observance of the culture, good things happen.

For example, leaders who expect their employees to be on time for meetings must also arrive a few minutes early. If the culture dictates that those meetings begin and end on time, the meeting coordinator must follow suit. A culture that encourages people to share industry-related news with clients and co-workers must be led by managers who pass along any articles of interest.

If the Companality values collaboration, actively seeking and welcoming the thoughts and ideas of colleagues anywhere on the org chart must happen equally from the top levels of the firm. And when someone's idea results in new revenue, a more efficient way of doing things, or a satisfied customer, credit must be given where it's due.

These behaviors by leadership model the positive elements of the culture, silently encouraging subordinates to do the same. As a result, the desired Companality is perpetuated. Of course the opposite can be true. When leaders violate the culture's standards, the whole Companality system erodes.

The personal example of a leader sends important signals to the members of an organization. This can be good news or bad news, depending upon how well managers model the culture, making the discipline of modeling of major importance.

Reward & Counsel

Employees learn to perform in culturally-compatible ways through either the rewards or corrective feedback that follow their actions. When a behavior is rewarded it is more likely to be repeated. And assuming that the employee was an appropriate hire, has bought in to the organization's Companality, and has been trained properly using all the methods available, an honest conversation about a cultural shortcoming, along with suggestions for improvement in the future, should not be a negative event.

As with every Companality element, leadership must be intentional about looking for opportunities to share pats on the back. The adage "Catch 'em doing something right" applies fully. Reward-worthy behaviors should be directly tied to some specific aspect of the organization's culture, which has been communicated repeatedly throughout the normal course of operations.

Of course managers can't be everywhere at once and have many other concerns on their minds, so programs that allow peer co-workers to bring positive actions to a supervisor's attention can be helpful. Even so, noticing stellar performances from employees, then handing out the rewards, must be a stated part of the boss's job.

The contemporary version of employee incentives has more to do with sincere recognition than dollars. Businesses with enlightened Companalities have taken note, shifting their emphasis from solely monetary to a more holistic mix of emotional and professional reinforcements. So while gift cards are never a bad idea, there are many other ways to say "Well done." Several of those are listed in the Companality Tools section of this book.

Behavior that is culturally contradictory can often be brought to an end by a simple discussion. Following certain best practices can make this a smooth and painless experience for all involved. By far the most important factor for ensuring that these corrective conversations are constructive is an accurate understanding of the word "confrontation."

Confrontation has become one of the scariest concepts in the English language. Very few people are comfortable with confronting a fellow human. This doesn't have to be the case. A true grasp of the meaning of this word can help immensely.

The word "Confrontation" has its roots in the 1630s. At that time its definition was "the action of bringing two parties face to face." There's nothing scary about that. In fact, it can even be enjoyable.

The more adversarial connotation is believed to go back only to 1963, referring to the Cuban Missile Crisis of the previous year. Sadly, dictionaries today often define confrontation quite negatively, ignoring the word's origins.

A mindset that views confrontation in its original form will enter a counsel-oriented meeting with positive expectations. The goal will be to bring the parties face to face in order to explore a recent event and talk about how it did or did not align with the culture. When a gap is uncovered, ideas for future improvements can be shared. It's a teachable moment without the baggage of judgment or punishment.

Other guidelines exist as well. For example, timing is critical. The interaction should take place as soon as the conduct or pattern is observed. Memories fade quickly, as do the concern over consequences of actions contrary to the culture. Connecting the discussion to the action, therefore, is essential.

Another key factor is confidentiality. Nobody likes to be called out in front of coworkers, even if the conversation is done properly. Due to workplace sensitivities and the possibility of harassment accusations, it may, however, be wise for managers to have a trusted colleague present. That person should be someone with whom everyone in the room is comfortable.

Ideally the discussions will be unemotional. If tensions do rise, and cannot easily be brought back down, thirty seconds of silence is often a good technique. Should this fail to remedy the situation, the session should be ended and rescheduled for some time in the near future, when the atmosphere can return to a state of calm.

It's also important to stay on topic. Digging up unrelated past events is unhealthy and only makes matters worse. Should that happen, the supervisor must bring the discussion back to the present situation. If the newly revealed issue is serious, it can be explored in a separate meeting.

Both rewarding and counseling are key Companality fortifiers. The pattern becomes an intentional, sustaining part of the organization's culture.

Be Consistent

Nothing undermines culture like inconsistency. That statement applies to all six of the elements discussed previously in this section on Companality Day To Day.

Perhaps you're convinced of the importance of appropriate staffing to maintain the desired culture. That's great. But one inconsistent hire can destroy the cultural dynamics of the team. So no matter how great the temptation to bring on someone who may not be a cultural fit, the thought must be resisted, and consistency must prevail.

When it comes to buy-in, everyone has to be on board. No exceptions. If an outlier is allowed to exist alongside those who believe in the culture, negative consequences will always occur. Hopefully, such employees can be brought into the cultural fold through honest confrontation. If not, a parting of ways may be the only solution.

The training that takes place in the conference room, at the water cooler, and in spontaneous interactions must always be on par with the desired Companality. The education about culture must never vary, and no training opportunities can be overlooked. The constant reinforcement of a consistent message speaks volumes.

Aside from highly sensitive issues, employees must never be caught blind-sided due to a lapse in communication. Such an occurrence can create an "us and them" mentality, with those team members who were left in the dark feeling unimportant due to inconsistent sharing of company news. They will then be much less likely to buy in to and stay excited about the culture.

Effective modeling, by definition, demands consistency. A person whose actions adhere to the culture today but not tomorrow is certainly not providing a good example for others to follow. Far from being a valued mentor, such an individual will severely weaken the Companality.

Rewarding good behavior will bring about more of that type of behavior. But when good behaviors go unappreciated, their frequency declines. Likewise, shortcomings in compliance with the culture, aside from the truly trivial, should always be met with a positive confrontation. If management turns a blind eye, it could be taken as an endorsement, or as favoritism of one person over another. Consistency in both respects, therefore, is key.

Consistency does not mean that the culture never changes. As discussed previously, should any element on the Companality Continuum need to be modified, thus affecting the Companality Vision, that's completely acceptable. It might even flag an improvement in the company. The process from there is the same as that stated throughout this section of the book (Companality Day To Day.)

Of course mis-steps can and will occur in any of these areas. An unfortunate hire, a team member resistant to some element of the culture, a failure to communicate or a leader who does something counter to the Companality Vision. When they happen infrequently, those are simply results of the human condition and not a cause for alarm. The person responsible, and sometimes the entire leadership in general, must be quick to acknowledge their shortcoming, apologize, and make it right.

Management must be uncompromisingly consistent in all elements and steps of developing organizational culture. Any lapses will leave people confused and create an impression that the organization is not taking its culture seriously. From there, it's a short step to a conclusion that the culture is not as important as they were led to believe, and a decline in the positive effects that the right Companality can deliver.

– – – – –

Companality Day To Day. Seven elements for developing the organizational culture your entity's leadership desires. Backed by a stated purpose statement, directed toward a Companality Vision which was plotted on the Companality Continuum. And now implemented throughout daily operations as the company staffs accordingly, gets buy-in, trains, communicates, models, rewards & counsels, and remains consistent. That's Companality in action.

12

Going The Distance

As we embark upon appropriate staffing, seek buy-in from every level of the organization, conduct training, communicate, model, reward & counsel, and work hard to maintain consistency, we learn along the way. These real-life experiences expand everyone's knowledge, including leadership. We find ways to improve the very cultural environments we ourselves have created.

With Companality – intentionally developed organizational culture – in the game plan, the team has an extraordinary capacity to overcome obstacles, achieving desired outcomes in line with your Companality Vision. Over time, the firm's reality will line up with the aspirations plotted on the Companality Continuum during your initial stages of intentionally developing organizational culture.

As employees discover the energizing effect of contributing to a corporate culture that suits their values and recognizes their efforts, they bring their best to work every day. They provide exceptional customer experiences through every step of the transaction, resulting in a customer following that identifies with that brand as an extension of their own beliefs and values. This brings a steady stream of exactly the type of clientele the firm wants. And each great experience inspires more of the same, causing the marketplace community to take notice. In time, a reputation emerges that is both accurate and solid.

This ongoing success comes as an evolving, step-by-step execution of a commitment to stand for something, set a course, and accomplish a mission. It's an approach driven by stated, agreed-upon objectives, and powered by the participation of people who embrace what they represent.

Maintaining an organization's culture is exciting, even fun, but it's not a walk in the park. The Companality may occasionally be challenged by any number of factors: a hiring mistake, a leadership mis-step, a momentary lapse in quality, or one of thousands of hurdles that arise in business. In most cases, if the culture was well-conceived, it will survive.

There are times, however, when it's necessary and appropriate to adjust something even as foundational as an element of the organization's Companality. If that happens, management must be bold and adjust all relevant steps of intentional organizational culture development – those described in these pages – as needed. And they must do it swiftly, without flinching in any respect. This is not an indication of failure. On the contrary, it can be a sign of growth.

The process of intentionally developing organizational culture is a self-perpetuating feedback loop. Once begun, it does not have a clear beginning or end point. And that's the good news, as the positive effects of attracting the right customers, attracting the right team members, and creating the reputation you want carry on indefinitely.

13

Companality Tools

Developing an intentional organizational culture, like any project, requires a set of tools. These can run the gamut from policies, procedures, meetings and events, to blog postings, e-mails, and communication vehicles of all types that make it easy to provide feedback. Of course, the Companality tools that are appropriate for one organization will be as unique as that firm's Companality itself. What works great for one entity may not work for the business across the street.

Here are some examples of tools and tactics that can be useful in facilitating ongoing Companality success.

New Hire Cultural Awareness Workshops

A formal cultural awareness workshop can be structured as a

half-day or longer on-site or off-site event where key elements of the culture are stressed along with real world case study examples. Presentations can be made by management, but perhaps an even stronger message can be sent if veteran rank and file team members who champion the culture do the sharing.

Seminars

Building a team that masters the Companality is a process. Only a step-by-step program can achieve optimum results. A seminar series with a facilitator who regularly conducts classes on key culture principles can provide valuable perspective and practical steps.

One-On-One Mentoring

As a complement to classroom seminars, one-on-one mentoring takes Companality instruction to a more personal level. An employee skilled in applying a specific element of the culture is paired with a co-worker who needs extra help with that principle. A ride-along or shadowing session of the two together provides opportunity for the trainer to observe and mentor. Ongoing interaction via e-mail, phone and/or in-person meetings can reinforce goals, track progress and evaluate growth.

Team Breakfast

Held on a regular basis, a team breakfast for employees can provide a low-key, low-cost opportunity to strengthen working relationships and promote the Companality. Over bagels, muffins, coffee and juice, employees can be recognized for outstanding work supporting and fulfilling organizational culture objectives. A short breakfast talk by a co-worker or member of management on an aspect of the Companality can stimulate fresh discussion and increase understanding and buy-in.

Display Board

A large, prominently-placed display board can be an eye-catching focal point for reinforcing the values of an organizational culture. It's a central place to post photos, clippings, customer testimonials, news of achievements by employees, etc. By regularly updating this highly-visible display, key elements of the Companality can be kept in the forefront.

Companality E-mails and Letters

E-mails and letters from a Companality initiative leader can provide timely news and information to reinforce various elements of the organization's culture.

Appreciation Calls

A call from a Companality leader to say "Way to go" to a team member who earned customer or co-worker praise is a casual but impactful way to underscore the culture. It's an opportunity to remind individual employees that they own the culture and encourage them to keep up the good work in delivering experiences that perpetuate it.

Appreciation Cards

Same principle as the Appreciation Call (see above) with a card signed by a Companality leader to say "Way to go" to a team member for delivering a positive experience. The card could even include a small gift – see below.

Gift Cards

A simple but meaningful token of appreciation, a gift card for an online shopping site, coffee shop or popular consumer brand can be given to any employee who performs a Companality caliber effort. No formal, pre-planned presentation needed, just a pleasant "Have a little treat on us" perk handed out in a spirit of sincere thanks.

Digital Lounge

A Digital Lounge can be set up as an online meeting place within a company's Intranet. Team members can post suggestions, ideas, questions and requests, and receive feedback from others. It's a platform that provides an opportunity to reinforce the Companality at every level of the organization.

Employee Recognition Programs

A vital Companality component is the development of performance metrics and incentive plans that encourage contributions to the organization's culture, and then rewards them. These programs should be active enough to stay on employees' radar screens, simple enough to limit administrative workloads, and flexible enough to change as needed in order to increase motivation levels going forward. Rewards can range from a special parking spot, trophy, gift card or cash bonus to a higher end item such as a digital tablet or road bike.

Friendly Departmental Competition

Similar to the Employee Recognition Programs described above, but on more of a team level. Which department best reflected the culture last month? Everyone there receives a gift.

And Much More

As you can see, Companality Tools run the gamut. Below are several more possibilities.

- Designated Companality Ambassadors or Champions within the company who initiate constant Companality efforts.
- An acronym that reflects key pillars of the culture.
- Posters around the office.
- Company blog with articles by management or team members who are heavily immersed in the culture.
- Company Color Day – Team members must wear some article of clothing with the company's colors.
- Lunch or dinner with someone from a high level of the company, such as the CEO, president, department supervisor, etc.
- A game that reinforces the culture.
- A Companality song.

- A Companality flag.
- A mascot.
- Contests.
- Videos.
- Companality Week – Activities each day that reinforce some element of the culture.
- A card printed with wording about the culture, for all employees to keep close to their work areas.
- Specialty items such as pens, mugs, caps, imprinted with a word or phrase about the culture.
- Town Hall Meetings, specifically for the purpose of fielding questions or concerns about the culture.

So many possibilities. The only real limit to the creation of Companality Tools is imagination.

14

Companality ... By Default, Or Intentional?

Every organization has a Companality right now. It's at the core of who they are as companies, government departments, non-profits, education or financial institutions, healthcare providers, dot.coms or any other entity or enterprise where people come together to serve a common purpose.

At this point, the definition of Companality that you saw at the beginning of this book will feel less academic and more understandable and relevant:

Companality is

a combination of characteristics shared across an organization that dictate the experience of both customers and team members as they interact with that organization.

Encompassing factors as philosophical as values, morals and ethics; and as practical as work spaces, schedules and dress codes, Companality can be a powerfully constructive or counterproductive factor in meeting the long-term goals of an organization. It affects the type of customers a business attracts, the caliber of those who want to work there, the firm's reputation in the marketplace, and its overall brand image.

For every organization rich in intentional culture there are thousands with cultures that have developed in an unplanned, reactionary way. These enterprises are shaped by factors disconnected from a cohesive cultural vision. Some rise to have their day in the sun, but often sink prematurely in a muddle of dysfunctional operational processes, apathetic personnel and missed opportunities.

Managers and leaders must decide: Do they want to keep the Companality they have and leave the future to chance? Or is it time to intentionally develop a culture that aligns with a well-defined vision and leads to a desired outcome? The answer to that question is not the end. It is the beginning.

15

Making the Companality Commitment

Picture your organization in a not too distant future, revitalized by an all new culture, a culture that meets the unique vision that you as managers and leaders carefully sculpted. It's affected the type of customers your firm is attracting; the candidates who apply to join your team; the morale of current employees.

And word gets around. Your company has the reputation you desired and set out to achieve.

What created this transformation? A commitment to developing intentional organizational culture. There was nothing haphazard here.

First, you became aware of a phenomenon known as

organizational culture. Just as a person has a set of characteristics that combine to form what is known as a personality, whole enterprises operate similarly. Attitudes, values, morals, work/ life ethic: all these are present in every business, non-profit, government agency, healthcare facility, etc., forming what can be called a Companality.

Further, you realized that Companality is consistent across entire firms, regardless of size or number of locations. It seems almost peculiar, but it's true. And you became convinced that the concept of organizational culture had far-reaching effects, both internally and externally.

You accepted the fact that every organization has a culture, including yours. But it wasn't the culture you as a leadership ever wanted. Although within the broad parameters of your industy, your specific culture had come about at the whims of strong-willed staff members, what people simply got away with over the years, and the way things were always done in the past. You were skeptical at first, but you eventually came to believe that it was possible to intentionally create an all new Companality for your business.

So you went to work. As a leadership, you brainstormed, discussed, took part in thoughtful and productive sessions among yourselves and with your team members.

You identified a compelling and inspirational purpose for your organization, one which reflected one or more ways in which your firm enhances the lives of your customers, and turned it into a written purpose statement. You plotted your ideal culture on the Companality Continuum, eventually arriving at a blueprint for the future. You called this your Companality Vision.

You put your ideas on paper and shared them throughout the organization. There were multiple meetings and discussions to ensure that everyone was on board and committed.

From that point, the mission was tactical. Selective staffing, getting buy-in from employees, ongoing training, open communication, disciplined modeling, motivational rewards, and constructive confrontation became common elements of daily operations. You used a variety of tools, remained consistent, and did all the right things. You made it happen.

Today the reality is evident as you walk the halls and interact with people at every part of the firm. It's a wonderful place to be employed, so you attract and keep a top-notch, hard-working staff. Your customers and patrons are loyal and refer you to others. The community has taken notice, and your firm now enjoys a stellar reputation and a flow of new inquiries via word of mouth.

You did it. You developed intentional organizational culture. Congratulations. Welcome to Companality.

# # # # #

Developing intentional organizational culture can be a much easier process with a bit of outside help from someone who understands. For customized consulting that can bring the right Companality to your organization, visit www.companality.com, or send e-mail to s.fales@companality.com.

Epilogue

If the concepts in this book have helped your life in any way, the greatest joy you can give this author is to live in harmony with those and pass them along to people you know.

And what you have heard from me,
commit to faithful men and women
who will be able to teach others also.

About The Author

Steve Fales describes himself as an ordinary guy with a desire to have a positive effect on everyone he meets. He and his wife Linda, who were married in their early 20s, live in south Florida and enjoy staying abreast of the adventures of their two grown daughters.

Steve is the founder of several small businesses, including an advertising/marketing agency with national clients. He maintains a rigorous physical training schedule in support of endeavors as a marathon runner and triathlete, and is an avid chess player. Through writing, presentations, coaching, and consulting, he communicates principles and techniques for personal and professional development and biblical spiritual growth.

Steve's life mission is to leave a legacy of having achieved his full potential and helping others do the same.

Steve Fales is available for public speaking, individual coaching, and organizational consulting. For information and additional articles similar to the ones in this book, visit the author's website/blog: www.twentythousandfeet.com.

Made in the USA
Columbia, SC
03 August 2019